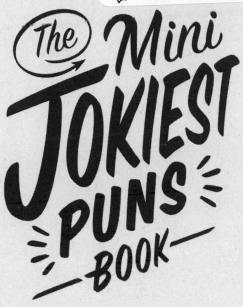

The Mini JOKIEST PUNS BOOK

JOKES BY **BRIAN BOONE**
ILLUSTRATIONS BY **AMANDA BRACK**

CASTLE POINT
BOOKS

THE MINI JOKIEST PUNS BOOK.

Copyright © 2020 by St. Martin's Press. All rights reserved.
Printed in the United States of America. For information, address
St. Martin's Press, 120 Broadway, New York, NY 10271.

www.castlepointbooks.com

The Castle Point Books trademark is owned by Castle Point
Publishing, LLC. Castle Point Books are published and distributed
by St. Martin's Press.

978-1-250-27035-1 (trade paperback)
978-1-250-27036-8 (ebook)

Our books may be purchased in bulk for promotional, educational,
or business use. Please contact your local bookseller or the
Macmillan Corporate and Premium Sales Department at
1-800-221-7945, extension 5442, or by email at
MacmillanSpecialMarkets@macmillan.com.

First Edition: May 2020

10 9 8 7 6 5 4 3 2 1

To Megan and Brendan, who
both enjoy my jokes and try to
out-silly me with their own.

CONTENTS

INTRODUCING . . .

Does something in here sound funny to you? We sure hope so, because we love silly puns so much that we put together this book of hundreds of the best puns of all time. Presenting: *The Mini Jokiest Puns Book*!

But just what *is* a pun, exactly? Well, call us a grounded aircraft, because we can . . . ex-plane. (Ha!) A pun is a joke that results from a clever twist of words, or a tweak of a phrase, or playing off the fact that one word sounds an awful lot like another word. The result: It ought to make you laugh . . . or groan.

Try this one out: What's the difference between a piano and a tuna? Well, you can tune a piano . . .

but you can't tuna fish! Get it? (We know you did . . . we can hear you laughing *and* groaning.)

Your friends, family, and classmates will love it when you brighten their day with one of these ridiculous, puntastic, puntactular, joke-ular jokes that are so packed with laughs they're huge-arious! We really think this is one . . . for the books!

Ready for some fun in the pun? Turn the page! (Or, if you're reading this at a library . . . check it out! Hey, once you get started telling puns, it's hard to stop.)

1
CREATURE FEATURE

**A teddy bear is a stuffed animal,
and this chapter is animal-stuffed.**

What do you call an alligator who wears a vest?
An investigator.

**It isn't a snail's heavy shell that makes it move
so slow. In fact, scientists have carefully
removed the shell to see if they'd be faster,**
but if anything, it made them sluggish.

Two silkworms had a race,
but they ultimately ended in a tie.

If you really need to get in touch with a fish,
the best way to communicate is to drop them a line.

A dog was arrested for giving birth on the side of the road.
Police charged her with littering.

What do you call a dinosaur whose vision is based on movement?
A do-ya-think-it-saw-us.

The farmer needed to move to a new farm, and he couldn't fit all the cows in one van,
so he called a mooooooving company.

That baby bird looks just like her father.
She's a real chirp off the old block!

Cows have to buy their cowbells and grass somewhere.
That's why they read a lot of cattle-logs.

Never, ever tell a pig your deepest, darkest secret.
They're bound to squeal!

You'd think clowns would be worried about sharing the circus with lions, but lions don't eat clowns.
You see, a lion tried to eat a clown once.
He spit them out because it tasted funny.

Did you know that there's a surefire way to catch a whole school of fish at once?
Just use some bookworms.

Why are there always ducks on the pond, no matter how early you go? Because they always rise at the quack of dawn.

Every day around noon, young cows like to eat their lunch together.
They do it in the calf-eteria.

A dinosaur crashed his car.
Talk about a tyrannosaurus wrecks!

Did you know that dragons are nocturnal animals?
They sleep all day so that they can fight knights.

Squirrels will usually run away from people, so how do you get one to like you?
Just act like you're nuts!

All the horses that lived next to each other in their stables were all very friendly.
It was a lovely neigh-borhood.

They say that it's impossible to make an octopus laugh, but it's just not true.
You have to tickle them ten times . . . ten tickles.

A puppy had never sat on sandpaper before.
When asked to describe it, she said it was "ruff."

What dinosaur knows the most words?
The thesaurus.

Why do bees have such sticky hair?
They use a honeycomb.

A farmer thought he had a really great dairy cow, but it produced no milk.
Talk about an udder failure.

Coral are sea creatures, but they do get stressed out.
Mostly over current events.

Why are cats good at stirring?
They bring their own whiskers.

The sheepdog counted 30 sheep, but the farmer only counted 28. Why the difference?
The dog rounded them up.

Never play checkers with the world's fastest cat.
He's a cheetah!

-ZZZZZZ

An awake dinosaur is a dinosaur.
A sleeping dinosaur is a dinosnore.

Did you hear that the frog left his car illegally parked?
It got toad away.

Did you see that film about dairy cows?
I don't think I've ever seen a better moooovie.

A dolphin strapped on a huge fake fin and swam near the beach just to scare people.
It could do a killer whale impression.

What do you call a snake that's 3.14159 feet long?
A pi-thon.

There was once a pony who was said to be a fantastic singer. But when she finally took the stage, she discovered she was a little hoarse.

A dog lost her tail, so she got a new one at the *retail* store.

Some fuzzy aquatic mammals escaped from the zoo.
It was otter chaos!

Dad: There are moose falling from the sky!
Mom: It's just reindeer.

The chicken leg approached its old nemesis, the beef steak.
"So, we meat again."

What's the difference between bird flu and swine flu, anyway?
One needs tweetment and the other needs an oinkment.

The champion race horse was made completely out of dough.
After all, it was a pure bread.

The buffalo's son went off to college.
So she said, "Bison."

Why do ants not get sick?
Because they have little anty-bodies.

Why did the octopus beat the shark in a fight?
Because it was well-armed.

What do you call a really tall cow?
High steaks.

What do you call a bear with no teeth?
A gummy bear.

What kind of car does a sheep drive?
A Su-bah-ru.

Smaller babies may be delivered by stork because they're small.
If they're bigger, they need a crane.

Do you like pig puns?
Personally, I find them boaring.

Why did the cowboy buy a Dachshund?
Because he wanted to get a long, little doggy.

How does a penguin build its house?
Igloos it together.

A fish walks into a restaurant. The waiter says, "Shouldn't you be in school?"

When will a horse talk?
Whinny wants to.

Did you see that horse that ate with its mouth open?
Such bad stable manners.

What did the momma cow say to the baby cow?
"Come inside, it's pasture bedtime."

Did you hear about the cat who ate nothing but lemons? What a sourpuss!

My cat sent me a letter in the mail.
She sent it furs class.

What do you call a horse and a bee that live next door to each other?
Neigh-buzz.

What do you give an alligator that needs help?
Gator-aid.

What do you get when you cross a parrot and a caterpillar?
A walkie-talkie.

One cat scared another cat.
"Don't do that!" the victim said.
"You freaked meow!"

This pet store down the street is having a bird-sitting contest.
No perches necessary!

What's another name for a sleeping bull?
A bulldozer.

My poor cat just threw up on the carpet.
I don't think she's feline well.

A duck walked into a department store, grabbed some tiny duck shoes, and left.
As he went out the door, he said, "Put it on my bill."

2
THE SPORTS SECTION

When you read these jokes about athletes and athletics, you're bound to have a ball.

How do archers get in shape?
They do arrowbics!

Golfers always wear two pairs of pants when they're out on the links.
Just in case they get a hole in one.

Boxers have a very dangerous job. They constantly put themselves in arm's way.

Race car drivers are often very hungry.
It's because they skip brake fast.

With the way they use those wooden bats, baseball players are really just lumber-jocks.

What do you call it when two wrestlers join forces?
A clobberation.

When does a baseball game start?
In the big inning.

A lot of people think Rafael Nadal is a really good tennis player, but isn't Roger Federer?

What's the difference between a baseball player and a dog?
The baseball player gets a whole uniform. The dog only pants.

What do football stars and waffles have in common?
They're both made on the gridiron.

I used to know this really funny joke about a boomerang.
I forgot it, but I'm sure it will come back to me.

The outdoors store was filled to the brim with people during its big paddle sale.
It was quite the oar deal.

A sports arena is a great place to spend a hot day.
It's full of fans.

That race car driver has had a very checkered past.

Why are soccer players so good at math?
They know how to use their heads.

What do hockey players and magicians have in common?
Hat tricks!

What's a runner's favorite class?
Jog-raphy!

Where do tennis players like to live?
Volleywood!

Why did the basketball player sit on the court and draw pictures of chickens?
She was trying to draw fowls.

What basketball player smells the best?
The scenter!

What time did the basketball team chase the baseball team?
Five after nine.

Why is basketball so gross?
All the dribbling!

I didn't think I was going to like soccer,
but as it turns out, I really get a kick out of it.

What do golfers wear on the links?
Tee-shirts.

If you're out camping and get cold, never build a fire in a kayak.
You can't have your kayak and heat it, too.

What kind of tea do hockey players drink?
Penal-tea.

Skydivers chute first, ask questions later.
It's no wonder they're so well-grounded.

Baseball is a team effort, especially those in the bullpen.
Everybody has to pitch inning.

People who do scuba.
Now there's a divers group of individuals.

I tried archery, but I didn't like it.
There were too many drawbacks.

A longshot was leading the big horse race, but not furlong.

Bungee jumping is an expensive sport.
Like they say, there's no such thing as a free lunge.

A fishing pole is really just a fish stick.

How did the baseball player lose his house?
He made a home run.

When the coach called in a new pitcher, it was such a relief.

Have you ever thrown a spitball?
No, and I hope to never get invited to one either!

Why do they play baseball games at night?
Because bats sleep during the day.

What's the first thing that a ball does when it stops rolling?
It looks round.

I didn't think I was going to like fencing, until I decided to take a stab at it.

First kid: Why is our tennis teacher so mad at you?
Second kid: He caught me raising a racquet.

What time does Serena Williams wake up each day?
Oh, ten-ish.

The bowling pins were tired of being mistreated.
So they went on strike.

What's the best time of year for jumping on a trampoline?
Spring!

We were going to tell you a joke about swimming, but it was too watered down.

Why did the ballerina quit?
Because it was tutu hard.

Why shouldn't you ever play basketball with pigs?
Because they're ball hogs.

Cinderella was terrible at sports.
Probably because her coach was a pumpkin.

Cinderella was terrible at soccer.
She kept running away from the ball.

Do you want to hear a story about a basketball player?
It's a tall tale.

What did the football coach say to the broken vending machine?
"Give me my quarterback!"

Did you hear about the extremely indecisive rower?
He couldn't pick either oar.

What got the martial artist so sick?
Kung flu.

Why didn't the dog like to wrestle?
Because she was a boxer.

A fish was arrested for swimming without a license. Police caught him and let him go.
That's when the fish said, "Whew, I'm off the hook!"

What's the difference between a baseball hit really high and a maggot's dad?
One's a pop fly, the other is a fly's pop.

What would you call a female goaltender standing between the two goal posts?
Annette.

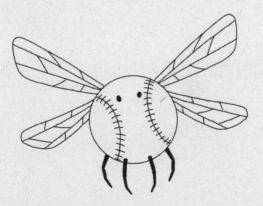

What do you get when insects play baseball?
Fly balls.

What's the difference between a fisherman and a bad student?
One baits his hooks, the other hates his books.

Why did the athlete want to buy nine racquets?
Cause tennis too many.

A really bad gymnast walked into a bar.

Volleyball players can always make extra money.
It's customary to tip a good server.

What's a banker's favorite track and field event?
The vault.

I lift weights only on Saturday and Sunday.
Monday to Friday are weak days.

What do you get when potatoes play baseball?
Fry balls.

What's the most important thing for a bunch of jokes about cities, countries, and places?
LOCATION! LOCATION! LOCATION!

Where do trees come from?
Oaklahoma.

Why'd they name it Wyoming?
Because wy not?

Did you know that Wisconsin has an unmarried daughter?
You can call her Miss Consin.

What state makes the most writing utensils?
Pencil-vania.

Did you know they made a sequel to Oregon?
It's called Moregon.

Did you hear the chocolate lover moved to Alaska?
He heard that it was full of mousse.

What state is always the most prepared and best dressed for sports?
New Jersey.

Why is there only one Arizona?
Arizona room for the one.

If there were only three more states, we'd have 53.
And then we'd truly be one nation indivisible!

What's the heaviest state?
Mass-achusetts.

Did you hear that the Italian airline messed up and forgot to charge a plane full of passengers?
They were free to Rome!

What's the fastest-growing city in the world?
Dublin.

Did you know that England doesn't have any blood banks?
Sure, but at least it has a Liverpool.

Her: Do you really think I'm from South America?
Him: Yes, I Bolivia.

What's the most fast-paced city in the world?
Moscow. Everyone there is Russian.

Lots of people want to visit the
Netherlands and buy clogs.
Wooden shoe?

What's the wealthiest city in Virginia?
Richmond.

Why is it called Washington, D.C.?
Because D C is just to the east.

There are so many lightning storms in Australia.
That's why they call it the land down thunder.

What's the oiliest place on Earth?
Greece.

What's the tallest building in your city?
The library, because it's got a lot of stories.

In which California city can you buy a really fancy Dodge Caravan?
Van Nuys.

Why is England so wet?
The queen has had a long reign.

Unless you visit Helsinki on your Scandinavian vacation, your trip remains un-Finnished.

When they told me La Paz was a capital city, I said, "I don't Bolivia."

Usually the only time CNN reports on anything in Norway it's Oslo news day.

Is there Nintendo in France?
Wii!

I went to a fancy English hotel.
Or, rather, a great Brit inn.

Where do the queen's dogs live?
In Barkingham Palace.

What state is great for dipping?
Oklahummus.

What state comes in a can packed with water?
Tunasee.

In what state would you find the most pigs?
New Hamshire.

Which state has excellent-smelling breath?
Vermint.

Which state is easiest to drive in?
Road Island.

When traveling to Central America, remember your manners.
Always say Belize and thank you.

I liked visiting Oceania, and I'd love to travel there Samoa.

She said she was from a country in the Middle East.
No, really, she's Syria's!

What's part of the United Kingdom and full of water?
Wales.

It would be fun to go the Emerald Isle.
Irish I could go this summer!

Why are French goats so musically talented?
Because they're born with French horns.

I can't wait to visit Africa.
I'm Ghana go later this year.

Want to go visit the most northern state?
Juneau you want to.
When I buy tickets, Alaska!

There's a giant country right above the United States.
Canada believe it?

I went to southeast Asia and it was so beautiful I felt weak Indonesia.

What Dutch city is full of cute and fuzzy rodents?
Hamsterdam.

Why are mountains the funniest place to visit?
Because they're hill areas!

What makes up the city of Boston?
About two thousand bospounds.

Never play Hide and Seek with a mountain.
They always peak!

**What's a better name for a food court when you're
on a diet?**
A craveyard.

What kind of music might you hear in space?
Neptunes.

What's another name for a dentist's office?
A filling station.

What do you call a hug in Paris?
A French press.

Where do police officers like to eat?
At the arrestaurant.

**A cruise ship is really just another name for a
boatel.**

Why are barns so noisy?
The goats have horns.

**What stands overlooking New York and sneezes
all day?**
The A-Choo! of Liberty.

What European monument can't stand up?
The I-Fell Tower.

Where do termites go on vacation?
Hollywood!

Where do wasps go on vacation?
Stingapore.

What's the world's laziest mountain?
Ever-rest.

What kind of hotels will birds stay in?
Anything cheep.

Where do shoelaces go on vacation?
Tie-land.

What's the best way to talk to Vikings?
You better learn Norse Code.

Where do shoes go on vacation?
Lace Vegas.

Where do pirates go on vacation?
Arrrrrrgentina.

What's the coldest place in South America?
Chile.

Where do viruses go on vacation?
Germ-any.

In what state will you find the most lions?
Mane!

What's the most popular game show in the ocean?
Whale of Fortune.

What state is the best to celebrate Thanksgiving in?
KenturKey.

What state is full of cats and dogs and hamsters and gerbils?
Petsylvania.

Did you hear about the kid who ran all the way from New York to California?
He needed to West.

Why was the horse from Kentucky so generous to his horse friends?
Southern horspitality.

Did you hear about the cheese factory that exploded in France?
There was nothing but des brie.

Did you hear about the crime in the parking garage?
It was wrong on so many levels.

Where do superheroes come from?
Cape Town.

What planet is like a circus?
Saturn—it has three rings!

What's the most popular pop in the Midwest?
Mini-soda.

They may look far apart on a map, but Ireland is just one C away from Iceland.

If you want to live in Australia and eat eucalyptus leaves all day, you have to have the right koalifications.

Why is Tel Aviv a great vacation spot?
Because it Israeli fun there!

My grandparents went on vacation to Cuba.
I hear they're Havana good time.

4
TOM SWIFTIES

"Tom Swifties are a very old and very fun type of joke," the book's writer said authoritatively.

"I'll go get the stick!" said Tom fetchingly.

"The number of people not attending class today really bothers me," said the teacher absent-mindedly.

"That *is* remarkable," remarked Tom.

"Have another cola," Tom coaxed.

"I enjoy hockey," said Tom puckishly.

"I'm returning to school soon,"
said Tom with class.

"I'm going to give you a haircut!"
said Tom barbarously.

"Hooray, another blackout!" said Tom delightedly.

"Here's your allowance for the next two weeks,"
Tom advanced.

"I'm here in your home for a visit," Tom guessed.

"You have the right to remain silent,"
said Tom arrestingly.

"I totaled those up for you," Tom added.

"Want to play cards?" asked Tom ideally.

"Hurray for our sports team!" said Tom cheerfully.

"I want a hot dog," said Tom frankly.

"May I join your singing group?" Tom inquired.

"I could use a pencil sharpener," said Tom bluntly.

"Shall I frost the birthday cake?" Tom offered icily.

"That's not _really_ Dracula," Tom discounted.

"I fixed the broken toilet!" proclaimed Tom, flushed with success.

"I just love adorable little bunnies," said Tom acutely.

"Fire!" bellowed Tom alarmingly.

"I can do that math really fast,"
said Tom calculatingly.

"Sure, there's room for one more," Tom admitted.

"Hey, I am so not full of hot air!" Tom belched.

"I'm a tailor," Tom panted.

**"I just got a job putting up steel girders!"
Tom beamed.**

"Look out for that bird!" cried out Tom, ducking.

"It's true, I chop down trees for a living,"
said Tom lumberingly.

"Let's get married," Tom proposed engagingly.

"Let's go shoot some hoops!" Tom bawled.

"Hey, what's it worth to you if I can help you escape from prison?" asked Tom contemptuously.

"The train's late," Tom railed.

"I've spotted more blackbirds than you have," Tom crowed.

"I've got to fix the car," said Tom mechanically.

"I only want to hang out with ladies," Tom mentioned.

"Dawn came too soon," Tom mourned.

"There's something missing from this flower bouquet," Tom said lackadaisically.

"Hey, use your own hair brush!" Tom bristled.

"I lost the debate when I ran out of things to say," said Tom outspokenly.

"The exit is right there," Tom pointed out.

"You snake!" Tom rattled.

"The eclipse is now starting," said Tom darkly.

"All right! I'm head of the refreshment committee!" said Tom, pleased as punch.

"Pete! Pete! Pete! Pete! Pete!" Tom repeated.

"Now I can do some painting," said Tom easily.

Where do baby spoons come from?
The spork.

Why did the computer crash?
It had a bad driver.

**What's loud, musical, and keeps sweat out of
your eyes?**
A headband.

What has four wheels and flies?
A garbage truck.

Why was the calendar out late Friday night?
It had a date!

How come the mail arrived wet?
There was postage dew.

What's a better name for a fly swatter?
A splatula!

I just read this novel in Braille.
It was a feel-good story.

That metal wire got so upset over some minor thing.
It got all bent out of shape over nothing!

I've never seen a fossil so opposed to doing any work.
Talk about a lazy bones!

Have you ever met that really funny sewing machine?
It keeps everyone in stitches.

What did the pencil say to the knife?
"You sure are looking sharp today!"

What did the paper say to the pencil?
"You have a good point."

It's time to sell your vacuum cleaner.
It's just gathering dust.

While it cost a lot of money at Halloween, that mask has no face value.

How do space cowboys see in the dark?
Saddle lights.

"Wow, look at that ceiling! What a great paint job! It's so high up there!"
–Ceiling fans

He didn't use to like masking tape.
Then he became very attached to it.

When I came across that big pile of free pants on the street, I really picked up the slack.

I was going to buy some thin sandals to wear on my beach trip.
But then I flip-flopped.

What did the kid say when his math teacher gave him a yardstick?
"This rules!"

Why did the woodsman put on pajamas?
He was invited to a lumber party.

Why did Miss Muffet need a map?
Because she lost her whey.

The kid's pants zipper broke.
But he fixed it on the fly.

What's round and angry?
A vicious circle.

I didn't want to know that she had false teeth, but some things come out in conversation.

What do brooms say to each other at bedtime?
"Sweep tight!"

What's another name for a grandfather clock?
An old-timer.

Who steals soap out of bathtubs?
A robber ducky!

What did the big bucket say to the little bucket?
"You look a little pail."

Why did the teddy bear turn down dessert?
Because he was stuffed.

Where does a power cord go shopping?
The outlet mall.

You should read this book about how boats are held together.
It was riveting.

A man went into a hardware store and asked to see some tools he could use to break up hard ground.
The clerk took him to a wall of shovels, hoes, and other tools.
He says, "Take your pick."

My mom gave some old rope a time-out.
It was being very knotty.

Have you heard the joke about the roof?
Never mind, it's definitely over your head.

Did you hear the one about the unstamped letter?
Never mind, you won't get it.

Want to hear a joke about paper?
Never mind, it's tearable.

Two houses situated next door to each other fell in love.
It was a lawn-distance relationship.

A nickel and a penny jumped off a moving train together.
But not the quarter. It had more cents.

I call my alarm "Jim."
That way I can tell people the first thing I do every morning is hit the Jim.

"Boy," said one shelf to the other shelf, "you sure look board."

Your fingers are a lot like the hardware store.
They've both got a lot of nails.

A beautiful marble statue decided to move off of her perch. She was tired of being taken for granite.

How do "Stop," "Merge," and "Yield" signs communicate?
Sign language.

Telling puns in an elevator is just wrong on so many levels.

Where do boats go when they get sick?
To the dock.

You can have my chimney for free.
It's on the house!

Why did the beams get together once a week?
It was their support group.

The teacher quit their job teaching kids how to do origami. Too much paperwork.

Did you hear that metal and a microwave fell in love?
When they met, sparks flew!

I asked my friend, Nick, if he had 5 cents I could borrow.
But he was Nicholas.

I bought a wooden whistle . . . but it wooden whistle.

He couldn't work out how to fix the washing machine.
So he threw in the towel.

If you buy a bigger bed you actually get less bedroom.

What vitamin will sting you?
Vitamin B.

These reverse-angle cameras in cars are great.
I got one and I never looked back.

The candle quit its job.
He felt burned out.

My phone has to wear glasses.
Well, ever since it lost its contacts.

People say I look better without my glasses on.
But I just can't see it.

If artists wear Sketchers . . . then do linguists wear Converse?

My new diet consists entirely of aircraft.
It's a bit plane.

"This job isn't for everyone," the scarecrow said,
"but hay, it's in my jeans."

Why are there fences on graveyards?
Because people are dying to get in.

Remember: Models of dragons are not to scale.

I owe a lot to the sidewalks.
They've kept me off the streets for years.

How do you keep an ig from falling off?
Igloo.

Towels can't tell jokes.
They have a very dry sense of humor.

I thought this old rope would be useful, but nope—a frayed knot.

Never trust an escalator.
They're always up to something!

That poor piece of paper pinned up to the wall!
It was under a tack.

Why did the smelter get arrested?
For steeling the iron.

There's nothing more odd than numbers not divisible by two.

Do houses wear clothes?
Sure—a dress.

A broken can opener is really just a can't opener.

I'm sorry you got hit on my way into the room.
Honestly, I a-door you.

A woman came home to find she'd been robbed of every lamp in her house.
She was de-lighted.

There's a wash basin standing in front of your door right now.
Just let that sink in.

Him: Does it seem weird that there's just one big factory that makes all the perfume in the world?
Her: Yeah, it makes scents.

What kind of shoes do ninjas wear?
Sneakers!

Here are some food puns to chew on . . . if you don't think they're too cheesy or corny.

There's only one way to fix a cracked pumpkin.
That's with a pumpkin patch.

What did the sesame seed say to the bagel?
"I'm on a roll!"

What's a good name for an almond in space?
An astronut!

A jar of pickles witnessed one of their own fall out of the fridge and onto the floor.
They just had to dill with it.

The bagel was made from the fanciest flour and other ingredients.
It was well-bread.

What did one plate say to the other plate?
"Lunch is on me!"

Did you hear about the sour orange that was expelled from school for being late?
The teacher got tired of how it was always tarty.

Newton's Law says what goes up must come down.
Cole's Law is thinly sliced cabbage with dressing.

Why do cowboys put big hats and boots on their salads?
They prefer ranch dressing.

Take the edible part out of a couple of bananas and what do you have left? A pair of slippers.

What do you give a lemon that needs help?
Lemon-aid.

I smeared some ketchup all over my eyes once.
It was a bad idea in Heinz-sight.

Why did the pie see the dentist?
It needed a filling.

Want to hear one about an egg?
Never mind, you wouldn't get the yolk.

Today we ate a pizza on the roof of the pizza parlor.
The manager said it was on the house!

The cool mushroom always got invited to all the best parties. Who doesn't love a fungi?

How do you make a tuna melt?
Pay it a nice compliment.

The scientist splt out her wad of gum when it ran out of flavor.
It was an ex-spearmint.

Boy: Have you ever eaten so many pintos and limas you get sick?
Girl: Yeah, I've bean there.

German sausages are the wurst.

Did you hear about the guy who got hit in the head with a flying can of soda?
He was just lucky that it was a soft drink.

What did one hot dog say to the other hot dog in the hot dog race? "I relish the fact that you've mustard the strength to ketchup to me!"

My little sister told me there's no way that I could ever build a bicycle out of spaghetti.
You should've seen her face when I rode pasta.

Did you hear about the cracker that went to the hospital?
It was just feeling crummy.

What nut are the most people allergic to?
Cashew!

Do you know why they sell sausages as links?
Because the butchers need to make ends meet.

There was a big sale at the fish market today.
Certainly there must be a catch!

Yes, I'm into fitness.
Fitness whole burger in my mouth.

There was once an army of pickles led by a brilliant pickle general.
It was a case of the brined leading the brined.

Boy: Some kid just came up to me and through a bunch of milk, cream, and cheese at me!
Girl: How dairy!

What's the difference between a pizza and pizza jokes?
Pizza jokes can't be topped!

Did you hear about the woman who quit her job at the doughnut factory?
She just got tired of the hole business.

If you want to have a successful luau, you're going to have to go whole hog.

Did you hear about the cat who fell into a pile of beans and wrapped itself up in a tortilla?
It was a purr-ito.

Did you hear about the guy who used to be a baker?
He enjoyed it, but he didn't make enough dough.

What do a weak cup of coffee and a cow that just gave birth have in common?
One is decaffeinated, and the other is de-calf-inated.

What do young Boy Scouts eat?
Cub sandwiches.

With all those pricklies on the outside, that one tropical fruit should be called a spineapple.

Why did they call it a salad bar, and not a veggie table?

What do you call an avocado with an electric guitar
A guac star!

What do a caramely candy bar and a cow's udder have in common?
They're both a Milky Way.

You can eat a sandwich any time of day.
It's always a square meal.

Did you hear about the kid who dipped his iPhone in caramel?
He wanted a candied Apple.

How do you make a lemonade stand?
Steal the lemonade's chair.

Did you hear about the 1,000-pound wad of bubble gum?
It was positively chewmongous!

You don't hear eggs telling each other jokes much.
Otherwise, they'd crack up.

If you want to laugh at these jokes about jobs,
well, you better get to work.

When you're named dentist of the year, they give
you a reward. It's just a little plaque.

**Did you hear about the woman who used to
be a train driver?**
She got sidetracked.

Never trust an acupuncturist.
*First they needle you, and then they end up stabbing
you in the back!*

Can I fill you in on my trip to the dentist?

My molars are really bothering me. Good thing
I have a dentist appointment today.
At 2:30.

Receptionist: Hello, please take a seat.
The dentist will see you shortly.
Patient: Thank you, I'm familiar with the drill.

After the police caught the burglar, they poured
cement on the culprit.
Now he's a hardened criminal.

Did you hear about the singer who got locked
out of her house?
She broke into song and couldn't find the key.

Santa's best toy-making elf left the North Pole and
started her own very successful toy company.
Now she's extremely welfy.

My grandfather is a baker, but he's never let me have his gingerbread recipe.
He said it's on a knead-to-know basis.

Did you hear about the pirate who covered his eye with sandpaper?
He was in a bit of a rough patch.

Pirates have a hard time getting through the alphabet.
They always get lost at C.

Why didn't the pirate take a bath before he walked the plank?
Because he figured he'd wash up on shore later.

After he quit pirating, the peg-legged pirate got a job waiting tables. At IHOP.

**"Yarr," said one pirate to another,
"what a nice wooden peg ye got thar. . . .
And such a shiny hook, too! How much did
they cost?"**
The other pirate said, "An arm and a leg."

What did the pirate say on his 80th birthday?
"Aye matey!"

Old carpenters don't retire.
They just lumber around.

**If you're ever searching for a job, the trick is to
look inside yourself.**
Then, it's all about the inner view.

What did the pirate say when his wooden leg fell off
during a snowstorm? "Shiver me timbers!"

What's the most tedious place in an office?
The bored room.

The pilot liked to be alone.
But even for him, flying a drone was just too remote.

What car would a farmer drive?
A cornvertible.

The failed poet decided to leave the writing to the prose.

We hired a tree trimmer and he did a great job.
He should take a bough!

What's another name for a happy cowboy?
A jolly rancher!

What happened when the worker rotated the heavy machinery?
He got cranky.

I got fired from my job flipping burgers.
Apparently I didn't turn up enough.

My brother got a job making telescopes.
Things are looking up!

Did you hear about the barista who quit her job at the coffee shop?
She couldn't stand the daily grind.

I was supposed to do a list of odd jobs.
I finished numbers 1, 3, 5, 7, and 9.

Did you hear about the skeleton comedian?
It was trying tibia little humerus.

A witch published a book of all her potion recipes, but it was ultimately useless.
She'd forgotten to run a spell-check.

When construction workers party, they raise the roof!

The ship's captain was expected to dock in a very tiny little space. . . .
He was under a lot of pier pressure.

We hired a door-maker the other day.
She really knew how to make an entrance.

My new girlfriend tends to bees all day.
She's a keeper!

What do you call a carnivore who also forecasts weather? A meat-eorologist.

The fishing company had a very catchy slogan:
"Yes, we can!"

A man sued an airline company after it lost his luggage.
Unfortunately, he lost his case.

I was accused of being a plagiarist.
Their words, not mine.

The "old woman who lived in a shoe" wasn't the sole owner.
There were strings attached.

A persistent banker wouldn't stop bothering me.
So I asked him to leave me a loan.

After years of hard work on the subject, the excited scientist finally unlocked the secret to human cloning. He was beside himself!

I hear that the post office is a mail-dominated industry.

A doctor broke his leg while auditioning for a play.
Luckily, he still made the cast.

The balloon maker had to close down her business.
She couldn't keep up with inflation.

Government leaders don't engage in surfing contests. . . .
It could set a president.

Kid: How do you like your job?
Garbage Collector: It's picking up.

I used to work as a hairdresser,
but I just wasn't cut out for it.

Why are kindergarten teachers so great?
They know how to make the little things count.

A scientist wanted to clone a deer.
So he bought a doe-it-yourself kit.

A man was fired from his job at the calendar factory.
Just because he took a couple of days off!

Barbers are excellent drivers.
They know all the shortcuts.

A ship carrying red paint shipwrecked.
It marooned all the sailors.

Why did the scarecrow get promoted?
Because he was outstanding in his field.

I know a tailor who doesn't mind making a pair of pants for me.
Or sew it seams.

I used to be a banker.
Until I lost interest.

Kitchen remodelers are very counterproductive.

A man heard that gold was discovered in Alaska. He immediately packed up his possessions and moved up there. Six months later, he gave up and went home.
It didn't pan out.

They buried the man in the wrong place.
Talk about a grave mistake.

Why did the man dig a hole in his neighbor's backyard and fill it with water? He meant well.

Patient: Doctor, my nose is running.
Doctor: I think it's not.

How do dog catchers get paid?
By the pound.

What do you call a student who always turns in their math homework late?
A calcu-later.

When the medieval warrior was awarded by the king, he was given a knighthood.
It was a big sir prize!

Policeman: Got any I.D.?
Lady: Got any I.D. about what?

What does a fisherman magician say?
"Pick a cod, any cod!"

What's the funnest candy in the world?
An entertain-mint!

Why'd they name it "television"?
Because "watch" was already taken.

Elsa and Anna couldn't get any money out of their bank.
Their accounts had been frozen.

I can't believe the movie had a tornado at the end.
What a twist!

Congratulations to Gaston!
He won the No Belle Prize.

Why was the Incredible Hulk such a good gardener?
He had a green thumb.

Why did the movie star put her house under a grove of citrus trees?
She wanted to live in the limelight.

What music does a balloon hate?
Pop.

Despite our hard work on our camping trip, we couldn't get the tent up.
Too many missed stakes.

Let's all give a hand to these sock puppets!

Some parents don't let their kids watch orchestra performances on TV.
They say there's too much violins.

I came home today and my piano was sitting on the porch.
It forgot its keys.

What's brown, wrinkled, and lives in a tower in France?
The lunch bag of Notre Dame.

The magician was driving down the street.
And then poof, he turned into a driveway.

Don't click the link in that guy's social media profile or you'll get a virus.
It's a bio-hazard.

There once was a poor actor who fell right through the floor during a performance. It was a stage he was going through.

Books That Should Exist . . . And Who Should Write Them

Put on the Brakes *by Sloan Down*

Mountain Climbing Dangers *by Cliff Hanger*

Growing Your Own Spices *by Herb Garten*

Dare Ya! *by Hugo Furst*

Good Tries *by Ernest Steffert*

I Bet You Enjoyed It *by Major Day*

Are Your Parents Doing Well? *by Howard DeFolks*

How to Be a Dog *by Ima K. Nine*

The Most *by Max E. Mumm*

The Least *by Minnie Mumm*

We're Not Done Here *by Morris Cumming*

Cooking with Shortening *by Chris Coe*

Playing with Fireworks *by Huell B. Sourry*

Why did the boys fire their slingshots into the air?
They just wanted to shoot the breeze.

Riding a Horse Without a Saddle *by Eiffel Downe*

How to Identify Cattle *by Brandon Iron*

How to Sing *by Mel O'Dee*

Dinnertime on the Ranch *by Dean R. Bell*

When Life Is Boring *by Dulles Dishwater*

Unpredictable Situations *by Mayer Mayknott*

The Story of Archery *by Bowen Narrow*

How to Make Fried Food *by Crispin Brown*

My Life as a Singer *by Mimi Mee*

Earrings *by Pierce Stears*

Census Methods *by Harmony Arthur*

Trick Airplane Flying *by Lupe de Loop*

Be Prepared *by Justin Case*

Jobs for Kids *by Hiram Young*

How to Get Your Blood Taken *by Amos Skeeto*

The Exploding Man *by Stan Wellback*

Hereditary Allergy Symptoms *by Constance Niffling*

The Heavy Load *by Aiken Back*

Demolition Derby *by Rex Carrs*

Stop Fidgeting *by Stan Still*

The Baker's Man *by Pat E. Cake*

Extra Innings *by Willy Won; Illustrated by Betty Wont*

The Worst Joke Book Ever *by Terry Bull*

That movie about the colander wasn't very good.
The plot had too many holes. I was straining to understand it.

Ever since he went to Neverland, Peter Pan just wouldn't stop flying around.

How did Darth Vader know what Luke was getting him for his birthday?
He could sense his presents.

Why was Dr. Frankenstein's assistant so enthusiastic to help?
He was just Igor!

How does Clark Kent keep the sun out of his eyes when he's flying around as his heroic alter ego?
A supervisor.

What do skeletons play in the band?
The trombone.

What does Superman like in his drinks?
Just ice.

Why does Superman get invited to lots of dinner parties?
Because he's a supperhero.

I don't care for Russian nesting dolls.
They're so full of themselves.

Have you ever tried going to bed with music playing?
It will give you sound sleep.

The show is called *SpongeBob SquarePants*, but everyone knows the star was Patrick.

Why do dust bunnies use computers?
To get on the linternet.

You can have these marionettes, free of charge.
Honestly, no strings attached.

Breaking news: Cartoonist lost in the woods. . . .
Details are sketchy.

Did you hear that they opened a restaurant on the moon?
The food was great, but there was no atmosphere.

News anchor: This just in: I'm holding a boat to a dock.

There's a new drama series coming on TV next week starring a pair of pliers.
I hear it's very gripping.

What kind of warts would you find on a space frog?
Star Warts.

I like fairy tales, but some of them have a tendency to dragon.

Not many people watch *Dumbo* anymore.
That movie is increasingly irrelephant.

Humpty-Dumpty may have had a miserable summer.
But hey, he had a great fall.

What happened when the guy dropped a piano into a mineshaft?
A flat miner.

Wile E. Coyote didn't go out and chase the Road Runner today.
He had a bad case of Acme.

What music does a mummy like best?
Wrap.

Who recorded all the exploits of the Knights of the Round Table for history?
King Author.

Did you see that movie about punctuation?
It was a period piece.

It's very hard to get a reservation at the library.
They're always totally booked!

There was a fire at the circus, and gosh, it was in tents.

You know why Waldo always wear stripes?
That way he won't be spotted.

What music does a boulder like best?
Rock.

Mickey Mouse helped his girlfriend buy a car.
She picked out a nice Minnie van.

Gosh, when my parents found out that I'd replaced their bed with a trampoline, they just about hit the roof.

Have you ever had a Chewbacca steak?
It's a little Chewy.

What's Batman's favorite sandwich?
Reuben.

Did you hear that Dracula was named the best bloodsucker of the year?
What a champire!

I just ate a bunch of Scrabble tiles.
My next trip to the bathroom could spell disaster.

The Invisible Man tried to lie to me, but I saw right through him.

Why does Godzilla rampage through the city and eat hotel rooms?
He has a suite tooth.

Did you know there's a 007 who spies only underwater?
James Pond!

Have you read the book about teleportation?
It's bound to get you somewhere.

I used to think I wanted to become a mime, but then I didn't think it sounded very good.

Did you hear about the human cannonball?
It's too bad he got fired!

Life, the world, and everything in it can be kind of punny sometimes.

What's a good name for a guy who works at a gas station? Phil!

When it comes to delivering her dialogue well, Anne Hathaway with words.

Which pop star makes rapid onstage wardrobe changes?

Tailor Swift.

Can you talk to your phone and ask it to do stuff?

No Siri.

Real Names of Hair Salons

Headmasters
Mane Attraction
Fort Locks
Shear Delight
Fresh Hair
Shear Madness
Blade Runners
Alive and Klippin'
Hair and Now
Hairoglyphics
Hair Necessities
Tortoise & The Hair

The Hairport
Cutting Remarks
The Mane Event
Cut 'N' Run
Curl Up and Dye
Hair On Earth
Headgames
Hair Today, Gone Tomorrow
Hair Raisers
Scissors Palace
Hairanoia

What's a good name for a kid who lives
in the bathroom? John!

Politicians with Amusing Names

Janelle Lawless was a circuit court judge in Michigan.

Jay Walker ran for office in Pierce County, Georgia.

Dave Obey was a congressman from Wisconsin.

Timothy Shotwell ran for a sheriff position in Clark County, Washington.

Krystal Ball ran for office in Virginia in 2010. She didn't win . . . but she probably should have seen that coming.

What's a good name for a firefighter?
Ashley!

Funny Beach House Names

Latitude Adjustment	*Surf 'n' Sound*
Once Upon a Tide	*Dune Our Thing*
Sea-Esta	*Shore Fun*
What's Up Dock	*Seaclusion*
Shore Thing	*Sunny Daze*
Family Tides	*Hide 'n' Sea*
Beachy Keen	*A Wave From It All*
All Decked Out	*Wait 'n' Sea*
Sand Castle	*Baywatch*
Gimme a Break	*Something Fishy*

What's a good name for a person with a car on their head?

Jack!

What's a good name for somebody who does yoga?
Matt!

What do you call a lady with a frog on her head?
Lily!

What's the difference between Christopher Columbus
and the lid of a dish? One is a discoverer,
the other is a dish coverer.

When the apple hit him on the head, Sir Isaac Newton understood the gravity of the situation.

Did you know that a chimp was once the president?
Ape-braham Lincoln!

What's a good name for a lady who wears a lot of red?
Scarlett!

What's a good name or someone who plays a stringed instrument?
Harper!

Truly there was no one in history who traveled and wandered around more than the Romans.

What do surfers wash their swim trunks in?
Tide.

What's a good name for a girl who lives on the moon? Luna!

A kid thought he was swimming in an ocean made out of orange soda.
It turns out it was just a Fanta sea.

Velcro is such a rip-off!

What's better in an emergency than an EMT?
A pair-a-medics.

Why did they call it the Dark Ages?
Because there were so many knights.

There was a robbery at the Apple Store, but they caught the guy because of an iWitness.

I, for one, like Roman numerals.

I changed my iPhone name to Titanic.
It's syncing now.

Who is the sleepiest world leader in history?
Nap-oleon.

What's a good name for someone who plays
the flute? Piper!

Why does the singer of "Chandelier" not want us to Sia?

Einstein developed a theory about space.
And it was about time, too.

Every car that isn't an Acura is technically an Inacura.

What does Adele eat for dessert?
Jell-O.

How did Adele treat her sunburn?
Aloe.

What's a good name for a tall girl?
Willow!

Paul Revere always carried tissues.
He was, after all, the town crier.

What did Benjamin Franklin say when he
discovered electricity? "I'm shocked!"

How much does a hipster weigh?
An Insta-gram.

I was trying to take a picture when my friend
ran up and slathered Vaseline on my camera.
Now that's what I call a photo balm!

Are these jokes about trees, flowers,
and the living world bound to make you groan?
Hey, it's only natural!

A's are a lot like flowers.
Bees follow them.

Did you hear about the belly button?
It was so smart that it went to school at the Navel Academy.

Did you hear the joke about the virus?
Never mind, I don't want to spread it around.

What's unthinkable?
An itheberg.

Why do trees make such terrible enemies?
Because they're the best at throwing shade!

Do you want a brief explanation of an acorn?
It's an oak tree, in a nutshell.

First Kid: Did you know that I can cut down a dead tree just by looking at it?
Second Kid: I know. I saw it with my own eyes!

What month do trees dread?
Sep-timber!

Take it from a scientist:
Never believe atoms. They make up everything.

The tree was very successful.
So much so that it opened up lots of branches.

What part of a flower can power a bicycle?
The petals.

What did the trees wear to the forest pool party?
Swimming trunks.

The campfire was nearly dying, but now it's
roaring again. "I'm stoked!" the fire said.

The trees were more than glad when fall and winter had both passed.
In fact, they were re-leafed.

There's no real way to tell if someone is color-blind.
There's a lot of gray area.

I'd tell you a chemistry joke, but I know I wouldn't get a reaction.

Groups of really intelligent trees tend to grow next to each other.
It's called a brainforest.

If you think it's bad when it's raining cats and dogs, you should try hailing taxis.

Two flowers decided to grow next to each other.
After all, they were buds!

What did the right eye say to the left eye?
"Between you and me, something smells."

They had a funeral for some boiled water.
It will be mist.

The clouds in the sky got so excited that it was spring that they wet their plants!

What's the best way to start a fire?
That's a subject that has been hotly debated.

No two people interpret colors the exact same way.
In fact, it's a pigment of your imagination.

What kind of trees do you get when you plant kisses?
Tulips.

What's the best way to impress an orchid?
Use lots of flowery language.

How come the little kid's tooth fell out?
Because it was looth.

Some astronomers were supposed to watch the moon rotate for 24 whole hours.
But then they got bored and called it a day.

How do trees access the internet?
They log on.

During the middle of a heat wave, our town got dumped with snow.
The weatherman says it was an ice-olated incident.

The earth's rotation really makes my day.

Only one large petal remained on the old rose.
Last bud not least!

Why are trees such big sports fans?
They just like to root!

Never discuss infinity with a mathematician.
They can go on about it forever.

What did the cowboy say when the varmint gave him flowers?
"What in carnation?"

Gardeners hate weeds.
That's because if you give them an inch, they'll take a yard.

How do florists make money?
By petaling their goods.

Why didn't the scientist give her mother flowers on her birthday?
She hadn't botany!

Why did the tonsils get all dressed up?
Because they heard a doctor was taking them out tonight!

During allergy season, it's best to wake up early and get all that snot out of your nose at once. Sneeze the day!

How do big mountains in cold areas stay warm in the winter? Because they're topped with snowcaps.

What's the top prize at a flower show?
A bloom ribbon!

I now know how gemstones are made.
The process is crystal clear!

Trees hate taking tests.
Those questions always stump them!

Trees are living things, and they get sleepy, too.
They occasionally need a nap—forest.

The nose was feeling very sad.
It was so tired of getting picked on.

Gardeners love their work.
Going to their job everyday is like a bed of roses!

There was a big natural disaster the other day.
The earthquake took the blame, saying "it was my fault."

Why did the piece of coal turn into a diamond?
It just couldn't take the pressure.

Why do geologists like their area of study so much?
It rocks!

In order for a fungus to grow, you have to give it as mushroom as possible.

If you want to make some money, get into flower sales.
Business is blooming!

People using umbrellas always seem
to be under the weather.

Most people prefer the summer to the winter.
And yet, snow happens weather you like it or not.

How do meteorologists greet each other?
With a heat wave!

How do clouds salute the president?
They hail to the chief!

The weather forecast called for freezing rain today.
And sure enough, it was an ice day.

Do you think plant puns are funny?
We're fern believers!

The moon saves money by cutting its own hair.
How? Eclipse it.

**We thought we "odd" to end this book
on something silly.**

Whenever you lie on the floor,
does it ever feel like the whole world is against you?

Do I have a time machine? . . .
Of course I have a time machine . . . .
I've had one for a long time . . . .
We go way back.

What school subject is the most shaping?
Geometry!

I've memorized 25 letters of the alphabet.
I don't know Y.

**I woke up this morning in the dark and forgot
what happens next.**
Then, it dawned on me.

No, I don't want to go shopping with you.
*Once you've seen one shopping center,
you've seen a mall.*

People who shed pounds are a bunch of losers.

**I'm afraid that my fear of moving stairs isn't
getting any better.**
If anything, it's escalating.

There was no reason why my glasses
suddenly fogged up. I was mystified!

Boy: I haven't slept for ten days.
Girl: Well, good! That would be far too long.

It seemed like Santa would be late this year, but he arrived in the Nick of time.

What do elves learn in school?
The elf-abet.

A man went to buy some camouflage clothes.
He couldn't find any.

Did you hear about the mind-reading kid who robbed a bank and escaped?
There's a small medium at large!

Ed's parents named his brother Ed, too.
Because two Eds are better than one.

Did you hear about the kid who wouldn't nap?
She was arrested for resisting a rest.

What birthday is your shortest?
Your twenty-second birthday.

Car repair should be called "autocorrect."

Don't tell jokes about being lazy. They just don't work.

Do you know sign language?
You should learn it, it's pretty handy.

The future, the present, and the past walked into the room.
Things got a little tense.

A man checked into the hospital covered in hay and riding a horse. Doctors say he's in stable condition.

Why don't some couples go to the gym?
Because some relationships don't work out.

What do you mean June is over?
Julying!

The alien spacecraft crash landed on Earth in an office supply store.
Finally, a UFO caught on tape!

I met some aliens from outer space.
They were pretty down to earth.

What's it called when you have too many aliens?
Extraterrestrials.

A girl went home to find a friend lying on her doorstep.
She said, "Oh, hi, Matt."

I had a pun about misplacement.
And then I lost it.

Why couldn't the dead car drive into the cluttered garage?
Lack of vroom.

Want to hear a pun about ghosts?
That's the spirit!

I really look up to my tall friends.

Q: What's the difference between a stamp and a girl?
A: One is a mail fee, and the other is a female.

A girl ran around and around her bed.
"What are you doing?" her concerned mother asked.
"I'm trying to catch up on my sleep."

This kid I knew was obsessed with monorails.
All he ever talks about is monorails,
particularly how they travel along a single rail.
He has a one-track mind!

I never thought I wanted a brain transplant.
But then I changed my mind.

Did you hear the joke about the town dump?
Never mind, it's garbage.

Who is bigger, Ms. Bigger or her baby?
Well, the baby is a little Bigger.

The prices on these cat foods.
They're meowtrageous!

What do you get when you cover a boat in slime?
An ooze cruise!

Why couldn't the kids go see the new pirate movie?
Because it was rated "arrrrrgh."

How long would it take you to count to infinity four times?
Four ever.

The cheapest way to travel is by sale boat.

Why did the man use the sauna?
He needed a boost of self a-steam.

I was in the statue wing of the museum not paying
attention when SMACK— I hit the rear-end of one.
That was when I hit rock bottom.

Why'd they call them "self-driving vehicles"?
Because "automobile" was already taken.

We all went to the reading of the will and found out what we inherited.
It was a dead giveaway.

What kind of dog drives a sleigh and comes once a year?
Santa Paws.

The cardiovascular system is a work of artery.
However, it's also pretty vein.

She had a photographic memory . . .
but she never developed it.

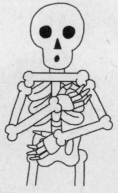

Why is a skeleton a bad liar?
You can see right through it!

Never spell "part" backwards.

It's a trap!

Did you read that article on ancient Japanese warriors?

If not, I can samurais it.

What rhymes with orange?

No, it does not.

Ten of these jokes were submitted to a joke contest.
Did any of them make the finals?

Nope, no pun in ten did.

How can you tell a vampire has a cold?
By his coffin.